COLLINS

RELIGIONS of the WORLD

written by
Elizabeth Breuilly and Martin Palmer

Note for parents and teachers

This fascinating introduction to world religions aims to give readers an understanding of different religions. While the book makes no claims for any one religion, it offers the reader the opportunity to encounter a variety of strongly held beliefs. Each faith is presented as accurately as possible within the scope of this book.

This book makes no claims about the truth or comparative value of any faith. If any statement or implication gives offence, this is entirely unintentional.

The authors have retained the convention of referring to years as AD (anno Domini – the year of our Lord) and BC (before Christ). Although this is a specifically Christian reference, and other faiths have other calendars, we wish to keep to familiar terms.

CONTENTS

Introduction
2

Buddhism
4

Christianity
10

Hinduism
18

Islam
24

Judaism
30

Sikhism
36

The Religions of
China and Japan
42

Religions in the
World Today
44

Religious Festivals
46

Glossary
47

Index
47

RELIGIONS OF THE WORLD

Every day, about 16,000 new Christians are **baptized*** or converted in Africa. Every week, over 10 million Jews throughout the world observe the Sabbath. Every month, around 20 new religious groups or **sects** start up in Nigeria. Every year, well over a million Muslims from every corner of the world make a special **pilgrimage** to a small desert town in Saudi Arabia – Makkah (or Mecca). They all do this because of religious beliefs. For many people around the world, religion is at the centre of their lives, and it guides their struggles and their hopes for the future.

Over three-quarters of the world's population is involved with a religion in one way or another. In Russia and Eastern Europe, since the fall of communism, **churches**, synagogues, mosques and temples are now full of **worshippers**. In South Africa, Church leaders, Hindu **priests** and Muslim imams work side by side to create a better society. But religious differences can create civil war and unrest. In former Yugoslavia, Israel and in many other parts of the world, religious disputes are causing pain and death.

For thousands of years, the religions of the world have been celebrating, teaching and telling stories of their faith. They try to answer the questions that most people wonder about

from time to time, questions like: *'Where did the world come from?'; 'Why do good people get hurt?'; 'What am I alive for?'; 'What happens after death?'* As far back as we can find, people have looked to religion to provide the answers. In the earliest burial mounds offerings to the gods are found and also preparations for life after death. In poetry from Egypt in 2000 BC there are questions about evil and about suffering.

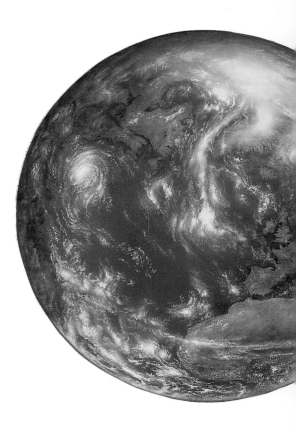

On the walls of caves in South Africa, Australia, Siberia, France and many other places, dramatic paintings have been found, which are tens of thousands of years old. These show how our ancestors went about their daily lives and celebrated their religion. To this day, some of the finest buildings, paintings, music and other works of art have been inspired by religious faith.

In this book you will find out about the major religions that exist in the world today and learn about their different customs and practices. You will discover what the Qur'an means to a Muslim; Divali to a Hindu; nirvana to a Buddhist and Easter Day to a Christian. As you will find when you read the following chapters, the religions of the world will always be fascinatingly different – in their beliefs, stories and ways of seeing the world.

* The meaning of the words in bold is explained in the glossary at the back of the book.

Buddhism

Buddhists follow the teaching of Siddhartha Gautama who left a life of luxury to seek an answer to why people suffer. He found the answer through meditation and became a Buddha, or 'Enlightened One'.

WHAT DO BUDDHISTS BELIEVE?

The belief of Buddhists is easier to understand if you look at the Four Noble Truths:

1 *That human life is full of suffering*
2 *That people themselves create this suffering because they are afraid to let go of their feelings; they try to hold on to the pleasures of life and they worry about being unhappy*
3 *That if people do not try to hold on to the things they like or avoid the things that cause them pain, suffering will cease*
4 *That the Noble Eightfold Path (see page 8) is a guide which helps people to let go, and eventually leads to an end of suffering*

HOW DID BUDDHISM BEGIN?

Siddhartha Gautama was born into a princely family in India near the border with Nepal about 560 BC. His father tried to protect him from the bad things in life, and never let him see any sadness or suffering. But when Siddhartha became a young man he went outside the palace walls for the first time, and was shocked by what he saw. He came upon a wrinkled, old man, a sick man, someone who had died, and a holy man who had given up all life's pleasures.

He saw how everyone, eventually, has to face sickness, old age and death. He knew how frightened people were of these events, and how their fear can make them suffer. He asked himself: was there no way to free people from this pain? To try to find the answer to this question, he left the comfort of his family and home to live as a poor man. He took the advice of religious teachers and disciplined his body by going without food, warmth and comfort, but he still could not find the answer to his problem.

Eventually, he developed a way of life called the Middle Way: he looked after the needs of his body, but did not seek any extra comforts or luxury. At the same time he learnt how to calm his mind by concentrating on breathing deeply. At the age of 35, on a night of a full moon in May, Siddhartha eventually found what he was looking for. As he sat under a

*The Sangha are Buddhist **monks** and **nuns** who have chosen to live as closely as possible to the Buddha's teachings. They keep his teachings alive, and rely on the kindness and generosity of others for their food and clothing. The Buddha was once asked by a king what a monk needs to be contented. He replied that a monk only has four basic needs for survival:*

1 **Food, which must be given freely**
2 **A set of three robes**
3 **Shelter for one night**
4 **Medicine for illness.**

Buddhist monks in Thailand.

*Siddhartha Gautama calmed his mind and body in **meditation**.*

The Buddha showed a path for all to follow. Buddhists followed in his footsteps

In the complete Thai edition, the Pali Canon fills 45 large volumes. It is divided into three sections known as 'pitaka' – baskets. The 'discipline basket' gives rules for the Sangha, the 'instruction basket' contains Buddha's sermons, and the 'great teaching basket' contains the most profound teachings.

tree, calming his mind with even breathing and meditation, he felt release from the pain of sickness, old age and death, and from the cycle of birth, death, and rebirth. He became a 'Buddha'– an **enlightened** one. For the rest of his life he travelled around India on foot, teaching and helping others to be free from the suffering that always comes from human needs and wants.

When Siddhartha died at 80 years old, he left his teachings – the Dharma – and he left his followers, organized into communities called the Sangha, to keep his teachings alive.

HOW DID BUDDHISM SPREAD?

Buddhism has spread far beyond India. It has helped to shape the lives and outlook of people in countries such as Sri Lanka, Thailand, China, Tibet and Japan, Cambodia and Burma, where the greatest number of Buddhists now live.

It is difficult to give an accurate figure for the number of Buddhists throughout the world, but it is thought to be in the region of 500 million.

WHAT IS THE PALI CANON?

At first the stories and sayings of the Buddha were passed down by word of mouth, as people related the stories and remembered many of Buddha's words. As time passed, it became more important to write down his teachings so that no disagreements would arise. These were written down in Pali, an ancient North Indian language which was probably spoken by the Buddha. 'Canon' means an agreed set of teachings.

WHAT IS NIRVANA?

Buddhists believe that when people die they are re-born into another life, time after time, still having to suffer and still wanting things. Buddha once said that it is like a dog tied to a post, who runs round and round in circles. The rope that ties people is the force of their own feelings and wants. If they hold on to greed, anger, desire, hatred and other bad feelings they

harm themselves or others by their words and actions. This creates a force called karma that ties them to the continuous circle of births and deaths.

But if people understand the Four Noble Truths and find a way to free themselves from all the sufferings of life, they can gradually cool down all their needs and wants like a fire dying down. The force of karma becomes less strong until it has completely gone. When all karma has gone they are free from everything that ties them to this world. This freedom is called nirvana, and it is the aim of every Buddhist to reach it, even if it takes many thousands of lifetimes. The Buddha passed on these teachings so that everyone can try to reach this ultimate freedom.

All Buddhists try to put aside some time every day to meditate, and a great part of every monk's or nun's day is spent in meditation.

HOW AND WHY DO BUDDHISTS MEDITATE?

Sitting in a comfortable position, the monk tries to calm his emotions and clear his mind. He may concentrate on a teaching of the Buddha, or on controlling his own breathing. This helps him to separate himself from the false hustle and bustle of ordinary life. By regular meditation, every Buddhist hopes to reach nirvana. In Thailand, the monks living in the forest spend three months a year, during the rainy season, in private prayer and meditation, completely alone.

DO BUDDHISTS BELIEVE IN GOD?

Buddhists do not believe in God the creator, or God as an outside force in their lives. The Buddha simply taught a path to freedom which can be followed by anyone. So Buddhists do not worship a god. But Buddhism uses the idea of gods as a way of awakening the 'Buddha-nature', which the Buddha taught is in every being. For example, statues or paintings of the gods of wisdom or kindness may be used in meditation to develop people's wisdom or kindness. In many countries, the Buddhism practised by ordinary people includes an array of gods, and the Buddha is sometimes worshipped as a god.

Sometimes Buddhists give offerings of flowers and food to honour Buddha. This shrine in Thailand is hung with garlands of flowers.

THE NOBLE EIGHTFOLD PATH

The Buddha taught that there was a path that anybody could follow which would help them overcome suffering.

1
RIGHT VIEWS
- to have a positive mind, to think of the good things in oneself and in other people.

2
RIGHT THOUGHTS
- to care for others, to be sympathetic and understanding.

3
RIGHT SPEECH
- not to tell lies, not to say hurtful or stupid things.

4
RIGHT ACTION
- not to kill or cause injury, not to steal.

5
RIGHT LIVELIHOOD
- to make sure that a job does not cheat anyone, or cause harm.

6
RIGHT EFFORT
- to work hard to follow the Eightfold Path.

7
RIGHT MINDFULNESS
- to be aware of thoughts and actions.

8
RIGHT CONCENTRATION
- this is the peaceful state of mind that should arise if someone has followed the Noble Eightfold Path.

WHAT IS ZEN?

In China and Japan, a form of Buddhism arose called Chen in China and Zen in Japan. When most of us think deeply about a subject, we think in words. When we want to understand or explain something, we use words. But Zen Buddhism teaches people that words are only the surface of things, and that you must try to get beyond words in order to understand fully the meaning of life. So followers of Zen may spend many years meditating on a sentence that appears to make no sense, and trying to understand what lies beyond it.

WHAT DOES IT MEAN TO BE A BUDDHIST?

Buddhists believe in reincarnation – that people have been born many times before and will have to pass through many other lives until they truly understand the Four Noble Truths and follow the Eightfold Path. Ordinary people can reach enlightenment, just as the Buddha did, but until they are ready for this they have to apply the Buddha's teachings in their day-to-day lives. The Buddha left five rules for everyday life, called the Five Precepts:

1 *Be sympathetic and helpful to all things that have life and be careful not to harm or kill humans or living creatures*
2 *Do not steal or take what has not been given freely by others and always be generous to those who are poor or in need*
3 *Never take more than you need whatever you are doing*
4 *Do not tell lies or say bad things about others*
5 *Never act thoughtlessly or carelessly*

Rule 1 is why many Buddhists are vegetarian.
Rule 2 is one of the reasons that Buddhists often give money to monks and nuns; the other reason is that the Sangha are preserving the Buddha's teachings to help everyone.
At the heart of the Buddha's teachings is the idea of not causing any harm to any other living being.

These rather puzzling sentences are used by Zen Buddhists for meditation:
Imagine the sound of one hand clapping.
What was your true face before your father and mother were born?

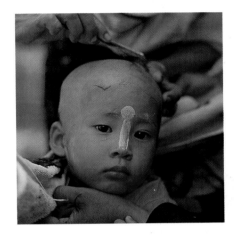

*In Thailand, all boys are expected to study and work on the land at a Buddhist **monastery** for at least three months. After this time, they are free to return home or to continue staying at the monastery. When the boy enters the monastery his head is shaved.*

The Buddha's footprints were one of the earliest symbols in Buddhist art.

Christianity

Christians believe that Jesus Christ, born to Mary and Joseph, was the Son of God. When he was born, the king tried to kill him, and the family had to escape into Egypt.

WHAT DO CHRISTIANS BELIEVE?

Like the Jews and the Muslims, Christians believe that everything was created by God. They believe that from early times, God has spoken to his people, trying to guide them and show them the right way to live.

Christians acquired their name because of their faith in Jesus Christ, the Son of God, who came down to earth to bring people back to God. They believe that there is a life after death which they can enjoy because of their faith in Jesus Christ.

This picture, from a monastery in Greece, tries to show God as creator and designer of the universe.

DID GOD REALLY CREATE THE WORLD IN SIX DAYS?

Christians learn from the Bible that God created everything in the world and continues to watch over everything and everyone. The first book in the Bible (the Christian's holy book), called Genesis – the beginning – describes how God made the world in just six days. On the sixth day he created human beings, and on the seventh day he rested.

Some Christians take this literally and think that the world is nowhere near as old as science claims. Many, however, accept the scientific explanation of evolution as a description of how God creates the world. The most important idea to Christians is that the universe is an expression of God's love.

WHO WERE ADAM AND EVE?

The Bible tells how God placed Adam and Eve, the first human beings he created, in a beautiful garden where everything was perfect and in harmony with God. But God made one condition, he told them they must not eat the fruit of the Tree of the Knowledge of Good and Evil. (Some songs and stories refer to it as an apple, but the Bible does not say this.) When Adam and Eve broke their promise and ate the fruit, they separated themselves from God and spoilt the harmony of creation. Some Christians believe that this event really happened, others view it as an important truth about the good and bad side of human nature. They say that it explains why human beings sometimes act foolishly, cruelly or selfishly.

The Bible tells how the angel Gabriel visited Mary, a young unmarried girl, and told her that she would give birth to a child conceived by the power of God. Christians greatly honour Mary because God chose her to be his son's mother and because of her unquestioning acceptance of his command.

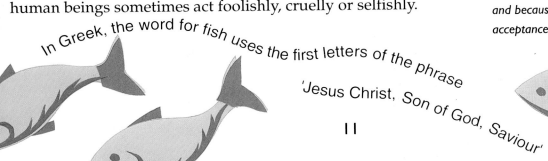

In Greek, the word for fish uses the first letters of the phrase 'Jesus Christ, Son of God, Saviour'

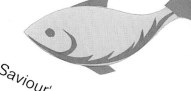

Many pictures of Jesus' birth show a manger in a stable surrounded by animals, but in the Bible only two Gospels, Luke and Matthew, tell the story. Neither mention a donkey, and only Luke mentions a stable. Matthew describes 'magi' (wise men from the East), but does not say how many. The number three comes from the three gifts that they brought – gold, frankincense and myrrh. The gifts were so valuable that people thought they were kings.

Christians celebrate Jesus' birth on 25th December, but no one knows exactly when he was born. The early Christians explained that Jesus' coming was like a light coming into a dark world, so they began to celebrate his birth at the darkest and coldest time of year.

The Western numbering system using BC (before Christ) and AD (anno Domini – the year of our Lord) is based on the year when it was thought Jesus was born. But recent research shows that Jesus was probably born in 4 BC not AD 1.

Christians trace through history how God tried to mend the broken relationship with human beings. In the Bible's Old Testament, God has a special relationship with the Jews. In the writings of the **prophets**, and the stories of such great figures as King David, Christians hear the voice of God calling to everyone to be sorry for their sins and to give him their love. But above all, God reached out to people by giving them his son, Jesus Christ, who in the end gave his life for them.

WHO WAS JESUS?

Christians believe that Jesus was the son of God. He was born in Bethlehem (now in Israel) to an ordinary Jewish couple, Mary and Joseph, around 2,000 years ago. He spent his childhood in Nazareth, but little is known or written of his early life.

WHAT HAPPENED WHEN JESUS GREW UP?

At the age of 30, Jesus began three years of travelling around the country teaching people about God, and healing the sick. Jesus began this public life by reading aloud these words from the prophet Isaiah:

The spirit of the Lord is upon me, because he has anointed me to preach good news to the poor. He has sent me to proclaim freedom for the prisoners and recovery of sight for the blind, to release the oppressed, to proclaim the year of the Lord's favour.

Jesus told people that this was the reason he had been born. He had a special concern for the poor and society's outcasts. Wherever he went, people came to listen to him and ask for his help. He chose 12 men, known as his disciples, to be his special companions and to travel with him.

Jesus' teachings upset both the religious and political authorities. They thought he was a troublemaker, and when Jesus rode into Jerusalem like a king, they decided it was time to get rid of him. They plotted to have him tried and executed.

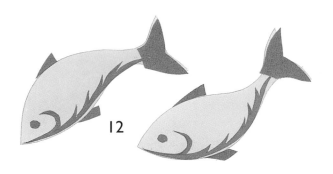

Judas Iscariot, one of Jesus' disciples, betrayed him to the religious leaders for 30 pieces of silver, and Roman soldiers found and arrested him. Although the Roman ruler, Pontius Pilate, did not really believe that Jesus was guilty of any major crime, a large crowd demanded that he should be **crucified**. On a Friday around the year AD 29 , Jesus was executed on a cross between two thieves. It seemed as if his life had been a failure.

WHY DO CHRISTIANS CELEBRATE EASTER?

After his death, Jesus' friends placed his body in a tomb cut out of rock and sealed it with a heavy stone. The next day, Saturday, was the Jewish Sabbath and no one worked. On the Sunday some women who were followers of Jesus came to the tomb to look after his body. They found the stone rolled away, and two men in shining clothes told them that Jesus had risen from the dead and they would soon see him again – alive. Over the next few weeks, Jesus' friends and disciples saw him many times, and they believed that he had come alive again by the power of God. This is known as the Resurrection because Jesus was raised from the dead to life again.

WHY DO WE HAVE 'GOOD' FRIDAY?

Good Friday seems a strange name for the day on which Jesus died. However, Christians believe that because of Jesus' death and resurrection, good triumphed over evil. Adam and Eve had disobeyed a loving God and brought suffering and sadness into the world, but Jesus willingly accepted his suffering and death to bring everyone back to God.

WHO IS THE HOLY SPIRIT?

In the forty days after his resurrection Jesus appeared several times to his friends and disciples. Before he left them for the last time, he promised that he would send a helper, a comforter, to be with them for ever. One morning they were all gathered in a room when they heard a sound like rushing

Jesus often told meaningful stories called parables. He once told of a son who had wasted his father's money and was afraid to go home. But the father forgave the boy and longed for him to return home. Jesus taught the people that God longs for each person in the same way.

The word Christ is not Jesus' surname. It comes from a Greek word which means Messiah in Hebrew (see Judaism page 31) – God's chosen one. Christians use the name to show that they believe Jesus is the true Messiah – the one sent by God.

In this picture of Jesus on the cross, painted in 1540, the artist has put in many details from his own time and his own belief. For example, Mary is shown dressed as a nun, although there were no Christian nuns at the time of Jesus' death.

By AD 180, Christianity had spread to all the Roman Empire and into Persia, North Africa, India and elsewhere. By 1300 it had reached Iceland, China and Russia. It then spread to Southern Africa, Asia and the Americas by European colonization. It is now the largest faith with over 1,700 million followers.

Christians generally meet together on a Sunday whether in a church, someone's house, a hall or under a tree, to pray and worship God. Through prayer and worship, Christians believe they get strength from God and learn more about putting their faith into practice. Church services can vary – there may be singing, quiet prayer, Bible reading and teaching about the Christian faith.

Many Christian families bring their babies to church to be baptized.

wind and saw bright flames which came and rested on each of them. All at once they felt a new power and courage and they knew that the helper had come. They rushed out into the street and told the people that Jesus had died, but had come back to life so that everyone could believe in the strength of God's love for his people. Christians believe that the same helper, the Holy Spirit, is with them all the time. He is God's power always at work in the world.

WHAT IS THE HOLY TRINITY?

Christians say that God is three persons in one: God the Father, who created the world, God the Son, who is Jesus Christ, and God the Holy Spirit.

Saint Patrick, the fourth-century saint who brought Christianity to Ireland, explained the Trinity by showing a three-leaved shamrock and pointing out that God is like the leaf – he is one person with three parts.

HOW DID CHRISTIANITY SPREAD?

When Jesus left his disciples for the last time, he told them to go out into the world and preach God's love and baptize people in the name of the Trinity. One of the most famous of the early missionaries was Paul, who had not known Jesus in his lifetime, but was the first to encourage non-Jews to become Christians. Soon Christianity spread from Israel around the Mediterranean, and to Egypt, Syria and beyond. But there was always fierce opposition to their faith, particularly from the Roman Emperors. By the year AD 100, 25,000 Christians had been executed for their beliefs, but their numbers still continued to grow.

WHO ARE THE SAINTS?

The earliest Christians used the word 'saint' to describe any Christian, nowadays the word has come to mean someone who is particularly holy or who is recognized for their special deeds after their deaths.

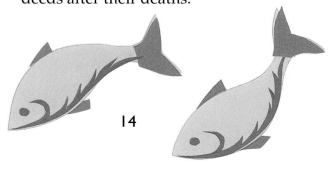

WHAT DOES IT MEAN TO BE A CHRISTIAN?

Christians believe that God wants them to be like Christ and with the help of the Holy Spirit, to carry on his good works in the world. Many Christians care for down-and-outs, the homeless or people who are rejected by society. Others work for peace and justice for all.

WHY DO CHRISTIANS EAT BREAD AND DRINK WINE?

Most Christian churches have a service, the highlight of which is eating some blessed bread and wine together. This service can be called: Mass, Holy Communion, Eucharist, the Lord's Supper. On his last night with the disciples before his death, Jesus celebrated a special meal with his friends. During the supper he took some bread, gave thanks to God for it, broke it and shared it with his disciples, saying, *'this is my body, which is for you. Do this in memory of me.'* Then he passed round a cup of wine, saying, *'this is my blood, which is shed for you and for many. As often as you drink it, do this in memory of me.'*

Ever since then, Christians have shared bread and wine, giving thanks for Jesus' life, death and resurrection.

WHAT IS IN THE BIBLE?

The Christian Bible contains: the Old Testament and the New Testament. The Old Testament has the same books as the Jewish Bible (see page 32). Christians understand these writings differently from Jews. The words of the prophets, for example, are seen as predicting the coming of Jesus. The New Testament has the writings about Jesus. There are four books called Gospels (meaning 'good news'), which describe his life. The Acts of the Apostles continues the story after the resurrection of Jesus, and tells how the faith spread. There are letters to Christian groups in different cities, teaching them more about their new religion. Several of these letters were written by Paul (see opposite). Finally, there is a book called Revelation, which vividly describes the end of time.

From the beginning, the breaking of bread has been meaningful for Christians. Immediately after the first Easter Day, two of Jesus' friends were walking along a road when a stranger joined them. They found his talk inspiring, but it was not until supper when he broke the bread that they recognized him as Jesus.

A priest repeats Jesus' words as he blesses the bread and wine.

On the night before he was arrested, Jesus shared a last meal with his disciples. Many artists have imagined the scene and tried to show how the disciples felt.

15

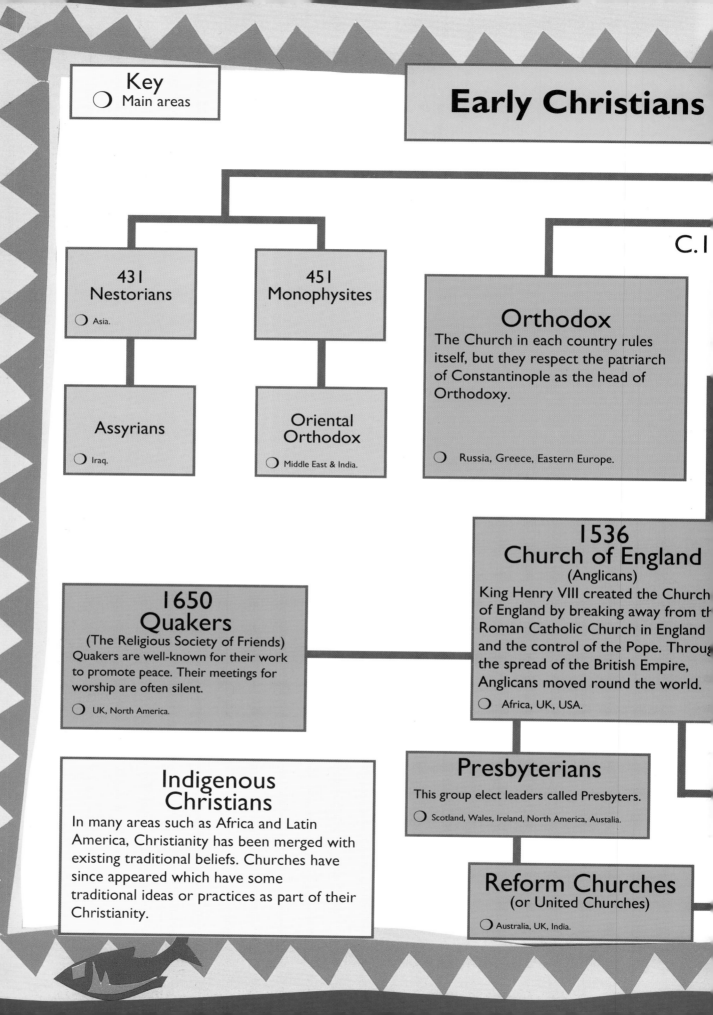

Key
◯ Main areas

Early Christians

C.I

431
Nestorians
◯ Asia.

451
Monophysites

Assyrians
◯ Iraq.

Oriental Orthodox
◯ Middle East & India.

Orthodox
The Church in each country rules itself, but they respect the patriarch of Constantinople as the head of Orthodoxy.

◯ Russia, Greece, Eastern Europe.

1536
Church of England
(Anglicans)
King Henry VIII created the Church of England by breaking away from the Roman Catholic Church in England and the control of the Pope. Throug the spread of the British Empire, Anglicans moved round the world.
◯ Africa, UK, USA.

1650
Quakers
(The Religious Society of Friends)
Quakers are well-known for their work to promote peace. Their meetings for worship are often silent.

◯ UK, North America.

Presbyterians
This group elect leaders called Presbyters.
◯ Scotland, Wales, Ireland, North America, Austalia.

Indigenous Christians
In many areas such as Africa and Latin America, Christianity has been merged with existing traditional beliefs. Churches have since appeared which have some traditional ideas or practices as part of their Christianity.

Reform Churches
(or United Churches)
◯ Australia, UK, India.

CHRISTIAN DENOMINATIONS

1184
Waldensians

○ Italy.

Roman Catholic

e Pope in Rome, Italy, is the head
the Church, and Roman Catholics
cept all his teachings. The Roman
atholic Church has many communi-
s of monks and nuns, which are
own as Religious Orders.

Europe, North & South America,
South East Asia, Southern Africa.

1517
Lutherans

Lutherans are named after Martin
Luther, an ex-monk, who began
the movement of protest (hence
Protestants) which split support
for the Roman Catholic church.

○ Northern Europe, Africa, North America.

1566
Calvinists

○ Switzerland,
Netherlands, Germany,
North America.

1580
Baptists

Baptists believe that people should only be baptized
when they are adult and old enough to make their
decision to be a Christian.

○ Russia, USA, UK.

Mennonites

○ Germany, Holland, North America.

1780
Methodists

John Wesley, an Anglican priest,
started the Methodists by reviving
Christian belief among working
people.

○ UK, USA, Polynesia, Africa.

Congregationalists

ey only make decisions as congregations.

Scotland, Wales, Ireland, North America, Austalia.

1830
Brethren

They try to live as close as possible to the lifestyle described in the
New Testament, and some (Exclusive Brethren) avoid contact with
the outside world.

○ UK, North America, South East Asia.

Hinduism

Hindus believe in one God who takes many forms.
Brahma, the Creator, arises from Vishnu, the Preserver,
at the creation of a new world.

WHAT DO HINDUS BELIEVE?

Hindus believe in one Supreme Being, or God, from whom everything comes. They say that God is like the root of a tree, and everything else in the world is the branches and leaves. Watering the leaves and branches will not do any good, but to water the roots gives life to every part of the tree. In the same way, if people want to do good for themselves or others, they must serve God, who is at the root of everything. One of their sacred books, the Bhagavad Gita, explains it like this:

'I am the taste in the water, the radiance in the sun and moon, . . . I am the sound in space, I am the strength in humanity. I am the sweet fragrance in the earth. I am the brilliance in fire. I am the life in all beings.'

WHEN DID HINDUISM START?

Some Hindus say their religion began hundreds of thousands of years ago. Certainly, some 3,000 years ago people in India were believing in God and worshipping in much the same way as they do today.

WHY ARE THERE SO MANY HINDU GODS?

'That which is one, the wise call by many names.'
Rig Veda

In the Hindu religion God has many ways of acting and ways of being known. For example, he creates each new world and each new universe. In this particular form, he is known as Brahma. But without God's action the universe could not continue, and God as Vishnu keeps everything going. Whenever evil threatens to take over the world, Vishnu comes to earth to fight against it. Hindus believe that Vishnu has come to earth 10 times in different forms, called avatars. Two of the best-known, and best loved, are Krishna and Rama. The story of Rama and his wife Sita is told in the Ramayana (see page 23).

The Hindu greeting, placing the hands together and bowing, is a way of saying, 'I bow to the spark of God that is in you.'

The name **Hindu** comes from the Indus river. When Western invaders, such as the Persians, arrived at the Indus river in present-day Pakistan, they simply gave the name Hindu to everything beyond the Indus.
The name has now been given to the vast array of different beliefs found in India.

Vishnu and Lakshmi, in their avatars of Krishna and Radha, are carried by the bird Garuda.

Each shape or movement of the hands expresses a basic Hindu belief

The god Krishna lived as a cowherd in the forests of Vrindavan in India. He was very handsome, and is often pictured with blue skin, which is supposed to symbolize beauty. The sound of his flute brought delight to the creatures of the forest and to the girls who looked after the cows. The Hindu festival of Holi celebrates the fun that Krishna brought, and his games and mischief.

In the holy town of Puri, the huge image of Krishna, called Jagannath, is displayed in a procession each year. Millions of pilgrims attend the festival, and Jagannath rides on a colossal chariot pulled by ropes. It is from this chariot that we get the word 'juggernaut' — meaning an unstoppable force.

When the world and the universe have come to the end of their present life, God takes the form of Shiva, who destroys everything in order that new life can then come out of the ashes of the old.

God is also known in hundreds of other forms, for example, Lakshmi: the goddess of wealth and the elephant-headed god, Ganesha: the god of good beginnings.

WHAT IS REINCARNATION?

Hindus believe that we were all originally part of God, but that we have forgotten our real nature and have fallen into this world of birth and death. They teach that we are part of the eternal spirit, called atma, without beginning or end. But atma, in this world, must be clothed with flesh and blood, mind and body, like an actor putting on a costume and make-up to play a part. When someone dies, the soul changes its body, changing the old costume for a new set of clothes, and is born again.

In each life, the atma makes good or bad karma (action). This karma shapes what form the atma will take on in the next life, and what part it will play. Hindus believe that in the next life people will have to suffer the results of their actions in this life, and they may even be born into a lower species of animals or plant. But if they live a good life, they will be rewarded in their next birth with a happy life.

It is not simply a question of reward or punishment, but the way things work, just as a hot fire will burn someone, so a greedy, selfish life will move a person to a lower place in the universe. Hindus teach that actions, once made, have far-reaching effects: for example, eating a hamburger means not only that a bullock has been killed for its meat, but it may also mean that a forest has been felled to make grazing land, causing the soil to become eroded.

WHY ARE HINDUS VEGETARIAN?

Most Hindus do not eat any meat or fish, and many do not eat eggs. This is because of their belief in atma and reincarnation.

Since all beings are part of the same spirit, they believe it would be wrong to kill a creature that is really no different from ourselves, but which is simply at a different stage in its struggle towards a better life. Hindus eat vegetables, grains and nuts, and also milk products. Hindus respect all animals, but to cows and bulls they give a special reverence. A cow cares for human beings: giving milk to be used for food, or to be made into oil for cooking and to give light. In India, the cows' dung is used as fuel for the fire, and bulls are used to pull carts and ploughs. The cow's gentle nature is seen as an example of how we should treat each other.

WHAT IS THE CASTE SYSTEM?

Traditionally, Hindus divided people into four groups, which they describe as being like parts of the body. The brahmins are the priest and teachers and are like the head; the kshatriyas are the soldiers and rulers and are like the arms; the vaishyas are the farmers and traders and are like the stomach; and the sudras are the labourers and craftsmen and are like the legs. Each of them has an important role to play but cannot do it without the others' help.

No group was supposed to be more important than the others, but in the course of time this idea hardened into a system in which people were forced into a caste just because they were born into it. Those who had no caste were then badly treated by everyone else. Instead of being a way to help everyone work in close harmony, the caste system has been used to keep people down and achieve power over them. Nowadays, many Hindus have relaxed or completely abandoned the strict caste system.

WHAT ARE THE HINDU HOLY BOOKS?

There are many sacred books in Hinduism, and different traditions rely more on some than on others. All of them are written in the ancient Indian language of Sanskrit, which is no longer spoken, but which is regarded as holy in itself. Among the most important books are:

When a Hindu dies, the body, like a worn-out piece of clothing, is cremated (burnt). The relatives may then scatter the ashes in a sacred place, such as the river Ganges, as a sign that they hope their loved one will be re-born in a higher existence .

*Hindus often have a small **shrine** at home devoted to one or two gods. The family care for their shrine, praying and giving offerings to God every day.*

Gandhi, the great Indian teacher and leader, was especially concerned at the way people with no caste were treated as the lowest-of-the-low. He campaigned to improve their position and instead of the name 'outcastes', he called them 'harijans' – children of God.

THE THREE MAIN HINDU GODS

Brahma the creator

Vishnu the preserver

Shiva the destroyer

BUDDHA

the teacher, is revered by Hindus as well as Buddhists, because he taught the practice of non-violence.

KALKI

the slayer who will come to bring this age to an end and destroy all that is evil.

MATSYA

the fish saved the creatures of the world from being drowned in a great flood.

KUMA

the tortoise helped the gods to become immortal.

KRISHNA

the cowherd is loved by humans and animals for his beauty, love and gaiety.

Hindus believe that Vishnu comes to earth ten times in different forms, called avatars.

VARAHA

the boar rescued the earth when it fell from its place.

RAMA

the king showed how to rule justly and live simply.

PARASURAMA

the warrior not only destroyed fighters but put an end to war itself.

VAMANA

the beautiful dwarf defeated the demon king Bali.

NARASIMHA,

half man and half lion, killed a demon who attacked Vishnu's worshippers.

1 *The Vedas*, which are the oldest writings. They detail how religious life and duty should be carried out.

2 *The Upanishads*, which are hymns and poems that ponder questions about life, creation, love and suffering.

3 *The Ramayana* and **4** *The Mahabharata* are two Hindu poems. The Ramayana tells the story of how Rama, a prince who was banished from his kingdom because others plotted against him, went to live in exile in the forest. With him went his wife Sita and his brother Lakshmana. But Sita was kidnapped by the demon king Ravana and taken to Lanka (modern Sri Lanka). Rama and Lakshmana, with the help of the monkey god Hanuman and his army, went and defeated Ravana and rescued Sita, then returned rejoicing to their kingdom. The Ramayana celebrates the strong love of a husband for his wife and a friend for a friend.

The festival of Divali in October celebrates Rama and Sita's return home. Hindu families put lights in every window to welcome them back to their own kingdom.

The Mahabharata is a vast poem about the struggles of two families over many years. In its crowded pages, the joys and pains of everyday life are acted out.

The most celebrated part of the Mahabharata is the Bhagavad Gita: the Song of the Lord. It is the teaching of the god Krishna to the nobleman Arjuna, just before a battle takes place. Arjuna queries whether it is right to fight. The Song explores questions like, '*What is our duty? What is our relationship with God?*' The Bhagavad Gita contains the heart of Hindu belief about life and about God's love for people.

WHAT DOES IT MEAN TO BE A HINDU?

The final aim of every Hindu is to be re-united with God so that they are no longer tied to the cycle of birth and death. The Bhagavad Gita gives three pathways to follow towards this aim: *knowledge* – to study the many ancient texts of Hinduism, think deeply about them and about the meaning of the world and the universe; *yoga* – exercises for both the mind and the body to help towards deeper and better meditation; *bhakti*, or devotion – to express and develop a love for God through prayer and service in many different ways.

Hindu temples are usually quiet, peaceful places, containing different images of God. People come at any time of day with offerings of flowers, food, or money for God. Through this worship, they express their devotion.

Islam

'If all the humans and spirits joined together they could not write a book like the Qur'an.'

These words from the Qur'an form the centre of this pattern. Muslims believe that the Qur'an contains the Word of God, revealed to the Prophet Muhammad.

WHAT DO MUSLIMS BELIEVE?

'There is no God but God, and Muhammad is the messenger of God.'

These words in Arabic are known as the Shahada, or the declaration of faith. A Muslim is someone who can repeat the Shahada, understanding and believing it fully. The word Islam means *'submission'* in Arabic, and a Muslim is one who submits his life to the one true God – Allah (in Arabic). Everything in a Muslim's life should be under God's control.

WHO WAS MUHAMMAD?

The Prophet Muhammad was born in Makkah, in the area known today as Saudi Arabia, around AD 570. Muslims believe that he was the final prophet, or messenger, sent by God to humanity. They believe that God had also sent other prophets, including Ibrahim (Abraham) and Isa (Jesus), but that the complete and final message from God was given to Muhammad. Because of this they give great honour to Muhammad, and when they say or write his name, they always add the words, *'Peace be upon him'*. But Muslims do not worship Muhammad; they only worship God.

As Muhammad grew up he earned great respect from people as an honest and skilful trader. One day when he was 40, he was meditating in a cave when he heard the voice of an angel. The angel gave him some words to learn by heart – words which called people to worship one true God. Muhammad was certain that this was a message from God.

HOW DID ISLAM BEGIN?

After some time, Muhammad began to receive further messages from God, and began to tell the people of Makkah. At this time people worshipped many different gods, and Muhammad's message was not well received. Many people thought that he was either mad or even evil, but others listened and believed in his words and began to pray to God.

Jerusalem is a sacred city for Muslims as well as for Jews and Christians. The most holy site for Muslims is the Dome of the Rock.

Friday is a special day of prayer for Muslims.

Muslims often use a small mat to kneel on when they pray. The top of the mat points in the direction of Makkah.

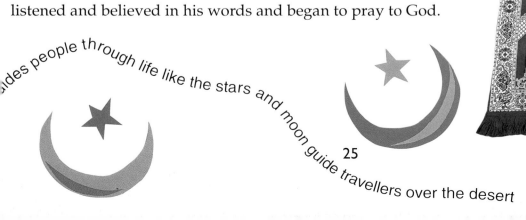

...des people through life like the stars and moon guide travellers over the desert

THE FIVE PILLARS OF ISLAM

These five special things that Muslims do are like the pillars of a great building, which support it and keep it firm and safe.

To believe in one God, and that Muhammad was his final prophet

To pray five times a day

To give Zakat, a part of personal wealth, which must be given each year to be used for charity

Every year, in the month of Ramadan, Muslims do not eat or drink during daylight hours

At least once in his or her lifetime, a Muslim tries to make a pilgrimage to the holy Ka'ba in Makkah

The non-believers made life so difficult for Muhammad and the other Muslims that they left Makkah and travelled to Medina, where they founded the first Muslim community. This was in the year AD 622. The Muslim calendar dates from this journey, known as the Hijrah. After a few years, Muhammad was able to return with armed supporters and defeat the army of Makkah to re-enter the city.

In AD 632 Muhammad died, but his followers took his message to many countries.

WHAT IS THE QUR'AN?

Throughout the rest of Muhammad's life he received messages from God. He learnt them by heart and then recited them to other Muslims, who also learnt them and recorded them on paper. Soon after Muhammad's death, all these written passages were gathered together in one book and carefully checked. This collection is known as the Qur'an (sometimes known as the Koran) and Muslims believe that it has everything that people need to know in order to live in Islam – in submission to God.

Muslims also look for further guidance in the Sunnah and the Hadith, which contain the sayings and actions of Muhammad while he was alive.

HOW DID ISLAM SPREAD?

A hundred years after Muhammad's death, the Muslims had defeated the great empires of Persia and Byzantium, and ruled from North Africa to the borders of China. In many countries people welcomed the Muslim rule because of its justice and religious freedom. Many of the conquered peoples eventually converted to Islam, although in some cases this took several centuries.

Now there are over 50 independent Muslim countries, and many other countries have a large Muslim population. There are probably around 1,300 million Muslims who live in the world today.

Muhammad and his companions spoke Arabic, and Muhammad received the Qur'an in Arabic. Muslims say that the Qur'an's language shows that it was given by God, as it is more beautiful than poetry. When Muslims read the Qur'an they read it in Arabic, and they also pray in Arabic. Muslim children who speak a different language at home usually go to classes in the mosque to learn to read the Qur'an in Arabic. Muslims say that it is the language of heaven.

In Muslim countries, when it is time for prayer, a muezzin ('caller') calls the people to prayer from the top of the mosque. The words are in Arabic, and they mean: Allah is most great; I bear witness that there is no god but Allah; I bear witness that Muhammad is Allah's messenger; Hurry to prayer; Hurry to success; Allah is most great; There is no god but Allah.

Soon after Muhammad's death, the Muslims disagreed about who should be their new leader, and they split into two main groups, which developed slightly different traditions over the years. The largest group became known as the Sunnis, and the smaller group (now comprising about 10 per cent of all Muslims) became the Shi'as.

WHAT IS SPECIAL ABOUT MAKKAH?

The city of Makkah is revered because it is where Muhammad was born and where he first preached God's message. But what is also important to Muslims is the Ka'ba, the first house of God on earth. Muslims believe that it was built by Ibrahim and his son Ishmael, and it is the direction they face when they pray.

The Ka'ba is a large square building, kept covered in black cloth which is richly embroidered in gold. In one wall is the Black Stone, a meteorite which Ibrahim used when he first built the Ka'ba.

Every year, Makkah is crowded with over a million pilgrims from all over the world. They walk seven times round the Ka'ba and visit other sites associated with the prophets. It is a time when Muslims from all over the world come together.

HOW DO MUSLIMS PRAY?

Muhammad taught Muslims to pray five times a day: at dawn, midday, late afternoon, evening and last thing at night. Before praying, they wash themselves carefully: hands, arms, face, head, legs and feet. It is a way of preparing for prayer and showing respect to God. When Muslims pray, wherever they are in the world, they all face towards the Ka'ba in Makkah. They use the words and movements that Muhammad taught: they stand up, bow, kneel, and then kneel with their face towards the floor. On Fridays, Muslim men meet in the mosque to make their midday prayers together.

WHY DO MUSLIMS NOT DRINK ALCOHOL?

The Qur'an gives directions for all aspects of Muslim life, including eating and drinking. The Qur'an forbids alcohol,

because it encourages quarrelling and makes people forget about God. The Qur'an also forbids eating anything from a pig, which Muslims consider an unclean animal, and any meat that has not been killed in the correct Muslim way, which involves saying the name of God. Meat which Muslims can eat is called halal.

WHAT DO MUSLIMS WEAR?

Muslims believe that modesty and correct behaviour between men and women are very important. Therefore both men and women avoid wearing clothes that are too revealing. Women usually cover their whole body apart from face and hands. In some Muslim societies they cover their faces in public as well. Men must be covered from the navel to the knees. Neither sex wears very tight or see-through clothing.

WHAT HAPPENS IN A MOSQUE?

Islam teaches that the whole world is a mosque – that is a place where Muslims can pray to God. All that is needed is an area of clean ground. But from the first Muslim community in Medina, Muslims have built mosques so that they can meet, pray and study the Qur'an together. The mosque also acts as a focus for the local Muslim community.

Every mosque has a main room for prayer, usually with a screened-off area for women, as men and women do not pray together. There is a washing area, and often a tower or **minaret** for the call to prayer.

Inside the main room, the direction of Makkah is marked by a small niche in the wall. When Muslims meet together for prayer they all face towards this niche. On Fridays there is usually a special sermon preached by the imam – the religious leader.

A Muslim wedding.
Islam's emphasis on modesty means that most Muslim families will not allow girls and boys to go out together, to chat or hold hands in the way that is commonplace in many western societies. Muslim parents see it as their duty to choose a suitable marriage partner for their children. Usually, they choose very carefully, taking into account the interests and background of the young people. Both the young man or woman can refuse to agree to a marriage that has been arranged for them.

The Qur'an forbids the use of images, or pictures, of living things. Instead, a tradition has grown up in Islam of making beautiful patterns instead. Sometimes they are based on geometric shapes, sometimes on plant shapes, and sometimes using the shapes of Arabic writing. The art of calligraphy – writing – is highly valued, especially using words from the Qur'an. This tile uses the names of the first four Caliphs (leaders) of Islam.

Judaism

The Jews trace their history back thousands of years,
and the Menorah, the seven-branched candlestick, is one
of their oldest symbols. In ancient times it gave light to
the Temple in Jerusalem. The central branch is said to
represent the Sabbath, the day when God rested from
creating the world.

WHAT DO JEWS BELIEVE?

Jews believe in one God who is the creator and lord of the universe. They believe that God has a special relationship – the Covenant – with the Jewish people. If they are faithful and live by God's laws, he will promise them a place in a perfect future world. Jews look forward to the coming of the Messiah, a great leader from God, who will bring a time of peace, fruitfulness and security to the whole world.

WHAT IS THE COVENANT?

The word 'covenant' means a solemn agreement. The Bible tells how, nearly 4,000 years ago, God made a promise to Abraham and his descendants: *'I will be your God and you will be my people.'* To the Jews this covenant means that if they were faithful to God and kept all his laws, then God would always look after his special people.

God repeated this promise to Abraham's son, Isaac, and to Isaac's son Jacob. God changed Jacob's name to Israel. He had 12 sons and the Jews are their descendants. In many of their festivals, Jews celebrate their history and remember the times when God has taken care of them.

WHAT IS PASSOVER?

At the festival of Passover or Pesakh, the youngest child in the family asks every year, *'Why is this night different from any other?'* At this time the Jews celebrate their ancestors' escape from Egypt – the Exodus. The Jews had become slaves in Egypt until the great leader Moses came to tell the Egyptian ruler Pharaoh to let them go. Time after time Pharaoh refused, and his country was hit by terrible disasters. At last, after the eldest son of every Egyptian family had died, the Pharaoh told the Jews they could go.

They left so quickly that they didn't have time to make proper bread with yeast, so instead they made flat bread. During the eight days of Pesakh, Jews eat flat bread. The high point of the festival is the Seder feast and service,

*Among the special foods on the Seder plate are a roast bone to remind Jews of the lamb **sacrificed** by their ancestors; a bitter herb (often horseradish) to remind them of the bitterness of slavery; a sweet mixture is included for the sweetness of freedom, and finally salt water for the tears that their ancestors shed.*

At the age of thirteen, in Jewish law, a boy becomes a man and is responsible for keeping the commandments. He becomes 'bar mitzvah' – which means a son of the commandment. He is also old enough to read the Torah aloud in Jewish services. When he reads for the first time, his friends and family all come to hear him and wish him well in his life as an adult. Girls sometimes have a 'bat mitzvah' ceremony – which means daughter of the commandment.

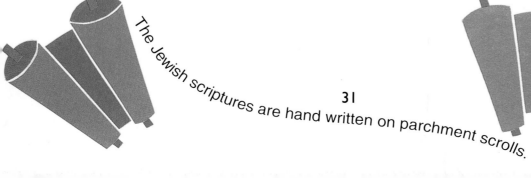

The Jewish scriptures are hand written on parchment scrolls.

Discussing the meaning of the Hebrew Bible is very important to Jews of all ages. The Mishnah (2nd century AD) and Talmud (6th Century AD) record the discussions of over a thousand rabbis (Jewish teachers).

The Torah is handwritten on scrolls which are kept in richly decorated covers. The silver ornaments include a pointer to use when reading the scroll, to avoid touching it with the finger.

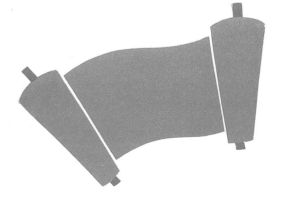

which is enjoyed on the first night. Families and friends gather for a special meal where the food, the table setting, the words spoken, and the songs sung all help to re-tell the story of the Exodus, starting with the questions from the youngest child.

WHAT IS THE TORAH?

After fleeing out of Egypt, the Jews wandered in the desert until they came to Mount Sinai between the Nile and the river Jordan. God called Moses to the mountain top and gave him the Torah: the first five books of the Bible containing rules for the people to live by. The most important of these are known as the Ten Commandments, but Jews also recognize a further 603 rules from the Torah, which help to guide their lives.

WHAT IS THE HEBREW BIBLE?

The Jewish Holy Books are found in what Christians call the Old Testament. They are written in Hebrew, the ancient language of the Jews. The most important part is the Torah which contains books called: Genesis, Exodus, Leviticus, Numbers and Deuteronomy. Orthodox Jews believe that these books were given by God to Moses.

The Hebrew Bible also contains the writings of the Prophets such as Amos, Hosea and Isaiah, books giving the early history of the Jews, and other holy writings such as the Psalms. These are poems and songs which express many different emotions: happiness, sadness, wonder, anger, praise, but they always speak to God as ruler of the universe. Many of the Psalms were written by King David, who grew up as a shepherd but became Israel's greatest king.

THE JEWS OUTSIDE ISRAEL

The Bible tells the story of how God helped the Jews to escape from Egypt and how he promised them a land to live in, which would be theirs for ever. After many years of wandering, the Jews reached a land near the river Jordan. They conquered the people living there and settled down in their new country. It became known as the land of Israel. King David made Jerusalem his capital city, and David's son Solomon built a great temple there for the people to worship God.

King David lived around 1000 BC. By 586 BC, Israel had been conquered and its leaders were taken away to live in exile in the city of Babylon. Although they were allowed to return 40 years later, many decided to stay in Babylon. This was the first time that the Jews lived in other countries. It took them until 160 BC to regain their freedom, but it was not long before they were conquered again by the Romans. In AD 66 the Jews rose up in revolt against their oppressors, but the Romans crushed them once again and destroyed Jerusalem. After this the Jews were scattered all around the world and had no permanent homeland again until the modern state of Israel was created in 1948. For many Jews, this land, and the city of Jerusalem, is the centre of their faith. They come from all over the world to visit the Western Wall in Jerusalem, which is all that remains of the last great temple.

Ever since the Jews lived outside Israel they have met together in synagogues to pray, to study the Torah and to help each other. A community of Jews may employ a rabbi to teach and help explain their faith. On the right of the picture you can see the curtain which covers the Ark, where the Torah scrolls are kept. The six-pointed star, or 'shield of David' is frequently used as a Jewish symbol.

WHY IS SATURDAY THE JEWISH SPECIAL DAY?

The book of Genesis describes how God created the universe and everything in it in six days. On the seventh day he rested, and the fourth Commandment tells the Jews to do the same. Sunday is seen as the first day of the week, so Saturday is the seventh, the Sabbath. Jews do no work from Friday evening to Saturday evening. The Sabbath is a day of pleasure, for family prayers and for celebrating the goodness of life through rest and refreshment.

BLOWING THE RAM'S HORN

In September or October each year, the Jews celebrate the birthday of the world at the festival of Rosh Hashanah – Jewish New Year. In 1999, the world is 5,760 years old according to Jewish tradition.

At Rosh Hashanah the solemn sound of the shofar, a hollowed-out ram's horn, calls everyone to prayer.

THE TEN COMMANDMENTS

I am the Lord your God, who brought you out of the land of Egypt, and out of the land of slavery.

1
You shall have no other gods apart from me.

2
You shall not make for yourself an idol in the form of anything in heaven above, or on the earth beneath, or in the waters below. You shall not bow down to them or worship them.

3
You shall not misuse the name of the Lord your God.

4
Remember the Sabbath day by keeping it holy. Six days you shall labour and do all your work, but the seventh day is a Sabbath to the Lord your God. On it you shall not do any work, neither you, nor your son or daughter, nor manservant or maidservant, nor your animals.

5
Honour your father and mother, so that you may live long in the land the Lord your God is giving you.

6
You shall not murder.

7
You shall not commit adultery.

8
You shall not steal.

9
You shall not give false testimony against your neighbour.

10
You shall not covet your neighbour's house. You shall not covet your neighbour's wife, or his manservant or maidservant, his ox or donkey, or anything that belongs to your neighbour.

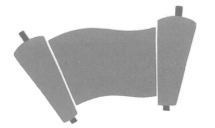

Rosh Hashanah is a time to think hard about the past year, and to be sorry for past faults. For ten days, ending with the festival of Yom Kippur, Jews prepare to make a fresh start in a new year.

WHAT DOES IT MEAN TO BE A JEW?

Jews base their daily life on the rules which were given to Moses. There are laws about almost every aspect of daily life. Some of these laws are about such things as being honest, being generous to the poor, or about health and cleanliness. Others reflect the Jews' belief that they are a special people because of God's covenant with them. Jews will not eat certain foods such as anything from pigs, rabbits or shellfish, and they prepare their food according to the law. Food that Jews may eat is called kosher.

There are many signs in daily life to remind Jews of God. Many keep their heads covered, often with a small skull cap, to show their submission to God. They may wear a tallit, a prayer shawl, which reminds them of God's law.

'Hear O Israel, the Lord our God is one God. You shall love the Lord our God with all your heart, soul and strength.' These words, known and used by all Jewish people, are called the Shema. The Bible tells Jews to keep these words on their foreheads, on their hearts, and on their houses' doorposts. During prayers, Jewish men tie boxes containing the Shema on their forehead and on the left arm near the heart. These are called tefillin. Jewish homes also have a box, called a mezuzah, on every doorpost. This, too, contains the words of the Shema. This boy is praying at the Western Wall in Jerusalem.

The home is the centre of Jewish celebrations. For the Sabbath and for festivals, the mother lights candles and sets the table with wine and good food. The family say prayers and blessings at the table and sing traditional songs.

There are two main groups in Judaism. The **Orthodox** Jews (left) keep to all the laws, follow them strictly and worship only in Hebrew. The Reform Jews were established in the middle of the 19th century and they interpret the laws more freely, worshipping in both Hebrew and their own native language.

Sikhism

The Sikh faith began with Guru Nanak who taught that everyone is equal before God. He said that if people pray and try to live a good life, God will be their Guru – their teacher.

WHAT DO SIKHS BELIEVE?

The basic beliefs of the Sikhs are best summed up in the Mool Mantra from their Holy Book – the Guru Granth Sahib:

*'There is only one God. Truth is his name. He is the Creator. He is without fear. He is without hate. He is timeless and without form. He is beyond death, the enlightened one. He can be known by the **Guru's** grace.'*

HOW DID THE SIKH FAITH BEGIN?

The Sikh religion began in North-West India in a region called the Punjab.

Guru Nanak, who first taught the Sikh faith, was born in 1469 at a place called Talwandi in Northern India, now in Pakistan. He was born in a Hindu family in an area deeply divided between Muslims and Hindus (see pages 24–9 and 18–23). Even when he was a child, people were amazed at the deeds he performed and the words he spoke.

The boy followed in his father's footsteps and trained to be an accountant, but even while he was doing his work his mind would often turn to thoughts of God. He and his friends often used to sit near the river and pray, but one day, his friends could not find him and they were afraid he had drowned. Then, three days later, he reappeared at his home. For one day he was silent. When he did speak he said:

'There is neither Hindu nor Muslim, so whose path shall I follow? I shall follow God's path. God is neither Hindu nor Muslim and the path which I follow is God's.'

What Nanak meant is that God is the all-important person and that it does not matter what religion you are. He went on to say that God had spoken to him and told him to go round *'singing God's song'*. He taught that religious ceremonies or formal praying alone do not bring people closer to God. If people really try to love God, and do what he wants, then God would make himself known to them and teach them how to be better people.

When Nanak was still a boy, his father gave him some money and told him to go to the nearby town and to trade with it. 'Do the best business you can,' said Nanak's father. On his way to the town, Nanak came across a group of men who were praying. They looked thin and hungry, and Nanak discovered they had not eaten for a week. He promptly went to the town market, bought baskets of food with the money his father had given him, and carried it back to the holy men in the forest. When he got home, Nanak's father asked to see what good bargains his son had made. He was angry when he saw that Nanak had returned empty-handed, but the boy explained to his dumbfounded father that he had done the very best business he could think of – he had helped feed the hungry.

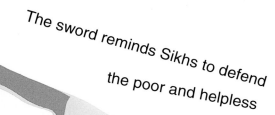

The sword reminds Sikhs to defend the poor and helpless

Men and women often take it in turns to prepare the langar – the meal that is served after a Sikh service. This is always vegetarian, so that all can eat it, no matter what their religious beliefs.

Sikhs today follow the example of their Gurus, and undertake hard work to help others.

WHAT DID GURU NANAK TEACH?

'God is the true Guru,' said Guru Nanak. He wrote hymns praising God, and these hymns taught people about God. For many years he travelled around India and other countries, singing and teaching. When he was about 50 years old he founded a town in the Punjab, called Kartarpur. Here many people came to visit him, learn from his wisdom, and to live as his sikhs – disciples, and so it was from then on that his followers were known as Sikhs.

Guru Nanak insisted that everyone was equal, so that no matter whether rich or poor, woman or man, prince or beggar, all should sit at the same table – something that was unheard of in India at that time. Sikhs today still place great importance on equality: men and women have equal status, and everyone, Sikh or not, is invited to a meal after a Sikh service. Both men and women work together to prepare and serve this meal.

WHO WERE THE GURUS?

When Guru Nanak grew old the Sikhs wondered who would become their Guru when he died. Guru Nanak decided not to choose either of his sons to be Guru after him, instead he chose a man called Lehna, who had followed him for many years. Lehna had always been willing to do any task that Guru Nanak asked him to do. He did not mind rough or dirty work, and he was always cheerful and humble. This is very important to Sikhs today: they do their best to serve others and often take on unnoticed or unpleasant jobs.

Guru Nanak changed Lehna's name to Angad, which means *'part of me'*. The name showed that Guru Angad was carrying on the same work and teachings as Guru Nanak. Before Guru Angad died, he chose his successor as Guru, and so it continued on. Each Guru chose the next one, and in all there were ten human Gurus. They guided the Sikhs by what they taught and what they did, and through the teaching of the Gurus, the Sikh faith grew and developed until it could stand on its own.

WHAT IS THE GURU GRANTH SAHIB?

The 10th Guru, Guru Gobind Singh, died in 1708 but he decided not to appoint a human successor. Before he died he said that the collection of hymns, written by six of the Gurus and by Hindu and Muslim teachers, was to become the people's final Guru. This book is now known as the Guru Granth Sahib.

It is treated with great respect, as a human Guru would be. A copy of the Guru Granth Sahib has a room to itself in a Sikh temple or at home, and normally rests on a special stand under a canopy.

Sikhs go to the Guru Granth Sahib to seek guidance, inspiration and comfort at various times in their lives. The book is read from start to finish during Sikh festivals.

The Guru Granth Sahib is treated with the respect that would be given to a living Guru. In a hot country like the Punjab, a disciple would stand by the Guru to keep insects and flies away. In the same way, whenever the Guru Granth Sahib is open, a Sikh waves the chauri over it.

WHAT IS THE KHALSA?

In 1699, Guru Gobind Singh called together all the Sikhs during the festival of Baisakhi. The Sikhs had been under attack for many years and life was very hard. Guru Gobind Singh called out for a volunteer who was willing to die for his faith – one man stepped forward from the crowd. The Guru took him into a tent and reappeared with his sword dripping with blood. In shocked silence, the people heard the Guru ask for another volunteer, and another man came forward. The same thing happened again until five men had disappeared into the tent.

Finally, the Guru went back into the tent and returned with the men who were all still alive. He had been testing the strength of their loyalty and faith in God. Guru Gobind Singh then announced that these five brave men would be the first members of the Khalsa – Sikhs dedicated to defending their religion and to caring for the poor and helpless of any religion.

Sikhs today decide when they are ready to join the Khalsa. It means a big commitment, so they sometimes wait for many years before they decide to join.

THE SIKH GURUS

The Guru Granth Sahib, the Sikh holy book, is the eleventh and final Guru

GURU GOBIND SINGH
1675-1707
Son of Guru Tegh Bahadur Founded the Khalsa, and declared that the Guru Granth Sahib should be the Guru after his death.

GURU NANAK
1469–1539
Founded the Sikh faith and wrote many hymns.

GURU ANGAD
1539–1552
Collected Guru Nanak's hymns and developed the script for writing them down.

GURU TEGH BAHADUR
1664-1675
He was martyred for preaching his beliefs that everyone should be allowed to worship as they wished.

GURU AMAR DA
1552-1574
Introduced Sikh festiva and several religious ceremonies.

GURU HAR KRISHAN
1661-1664
Son of Guru Har Rai He was only five years old when he became Guru, and he died three years later, after caring for smallpox victims.

The ten human Gurus, shown with haloes, are pictured with two attendants.

GURU RAM DA
1574-1581
Founded the town o Amritsar, and dug the p by which the holy Gold Temple stands.

GURU HAR RAI
1644-1661
Grandson of Guru Hargobind opened hospitals where medical treatment was given free.

GURU HARGOBIND
1606-1644
Son of Guru Arjan. Developed government and ways of living based on Sikh teachings.

GURU ARJAN
1581-1606
Son of Guru Ram Das Collected hymns of previous Gurus into one book. Built the Golden Temple. He was martyred for his faith.

WHY DO SIKHS DRESS IN A SPECIAL WAY?

All Sikhs wear five symbols which can be called the uniform of their faith. These were all chosen by Guru Gobind Singh. As these all begin with the letter 'K' in the Punjabi language, they are known as the Five Ks. The five signs are: uncut hair (kesh); the comb (kanga) to keep the hair clean and tidy; the steel wrist band (kara) which reminds Sikhs that God is one, without beginning or end; the sword (kirpan) to defend the faith and the poor and helpless, and the short trousers (kaccha or kacchera) which make it easier to move about.

The turban is not one of the five Ks, but it covers the long, uncut hair and keeps it in place. Guru Gobind Singh wore a turban, and his followers copied him, wishing to be like him in every way.

Sikhs wearing the 5Ks.

WHY DO SO MANY SIKHS HAVE THE SAME SURNAME?

Guru Gobind Singh changed the names of all the Sikhs to show that they now belonged to one big family. He told men they were to have the surname Singh, meaning lion, and the women were to have the surname Kaur, meaning princess. Sikhs still use these names, but sometimes they add a family name as well to avoid confusion for other people.

WHERE DO SIKHS WORSHIP?

The Sikh place of worship is called the Gurdwara – the door of the Guru. The Gurdwara is not just a place to keep the Guru Granth Sahib and to hold services. It is also a community centre and has a langar, or free kitchen, in it where anyone who is hungry can come and be fed. The most famous and holy of the Sikh temples is the Golden Temple at Amritsar in the Punjab. The oldest copy of the Guru Granth Sahib is kept in this temple and many Sikhs make a pilgrimage to visit it.

The Golden Temple is surrounded by a pool of water and approached by a causeway.

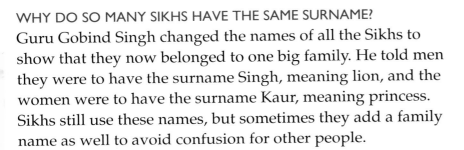

*A shrine to Lao Tzu, who lived in the 6th century BC. Taoists believe that by studying his writings they can become part of the Way of the Universe and become **immortal**.*

In most traditional Chinese homes, the family worship in front of a tablet with the names of their ancestors written upon it.

The dragon dance at Chinese New Year is performed to bring good fortune to all in the city – in this case Manchester, England.

THE RELIGIONS OF CHINA AND JAPAN

CHINA

China has been a communist country for 40 years now, and the government has controlled and discouraged any following of religion. But within China, there are practising Buddhists, Christians, Muslims and many other faiths. However, many Chinese combine teachings, gods and beliefs from three different religions of ancient China: Confucianism, Taoism and Buddhism.

WHAT DID CONFUCIUS SAY?

Confucianism is named after a great philosopher called K'ung Fu Tzu, who is known as Confucius in English. He lived in the 6th century BC and he tried to get the kings and governments of his time to be good rulers and to care for their subjects. No one took much notice of his teachings at the time, but over the centuries after his death, people gradually accepted his ideas. He taught that everyone had a proper place in society: children should obey their parents; wives should obey their husbands; the people should obey the emperor; the emperor should obey Heaven. He said that if everyone knew their place and behaved well, then the state would run properly. For over two thousand years his teachings guided and shaped the Chinese government and how Chinese families lived. The worship of ancestors became a very important part of Chinese life. They felt that if they showed respect to their elders and ancestors they would receive their blessings.

WHAT IS 'THE WAY'?

Taoism is probably the oldest Chinese religion. It is called Taoism because of the Chinese word *'Tao'*, which means *'The Way'*. Taoists believe that if you follow the true Way, you can live in harmony with the forces of the universe. Popular Taoism is found in many Chinese homes worldwide.

Here Taoism is used as a powerful force for fighting evil spirits, protecting the young, healing the sick or for guiding everyday life. Taoists see the world as being full of spirits, and they use special charms and chants to call upon the spirit world to help protect their family or even the world.

BUDDHISM IN CHINA

China created various new forms of Buddhism. One of the most famous is Chen Buddhism, which later went to Japan and became Zen Buddhism (see page 9). But there is also a popular kind of Buddhism which, like Taoism, uses charms and chants to protect against misfortune. With this Buddhism gods and goddesses are very important.

Kuan Yin, goddess of Mercy, is the most popular of the Chinese gods and goddesses. There are many stories told of how she has helped people with problems, and people pray to her when they are in difficulties.

JAPAN

The oldest religion of Japan is Shintoism, which means the Way of the Gods. Shintoism is closely linked to nature's seasons and the harvests. For Shintoists, the land of Japan is full of the spirits of nature. All over Japan you can find Shinto shrines, usually in the centre of beautiful groves of trees or situated on wooded hills.

BUDDHISM IN JAPAN

Buddhism came to Japan from China. In Japan, Buddhism developed many new forms, such as Zen Buddhism (see page 9). Pure Land Buddhism is also of Japanese origin. Instead of the many lifetimes of meditation needed to reach nirvana and freedom from suffering, Pure Land Buddhism teaches that all you need is to believe in the true Buddha – Amida Buddha – and call on him for his help.

Many Japanese would call themselves Buddhists, but they also practise Shinto rituals and celebrate Shinto festivals.

A Shinto temple in Kyoto. The most famous Shinto shrines, where it is believed heaven and earth meet, are on either side of the river Isuzu. All Shintoists hope to make a pilgrimage here once in their lifetime.

Ying and yang are the two opposite forces in the universe, like winter and summer

RELIGION IN THE WORLD TODAY

All over the world, religion is a powerful force for hundreds of millions of people. Often its power can help people in difficulties. In some poorer areas of the world where there is hunger, war or a natural disaster has struck, religious aid agencies like Christian Aid or Muslim Aid work with the people there and bring much needed provisions, food and clothing. They will help rebuild homes and lives and look for ways to prevent these disasters happening again. In many countries, religious organizations work hard to try to make their governments listen to the poor and the helpless.

WHAT CAUSES RELIGIOUS WARS?

Sometimes, religion can be destructive. In Northern Ireland the feud between the Roman Catholics and the Protestants caused violence for centuries. In the Sudan, problems and disagreements between the Muslims in the north and the Christians in the south have led to civil war. In Sri Lanka, fighting between Buddhists and Hindus has turned much of the northern tip of the island into a war zone.

In the past, the different religions and groups often had little to do with each other. Some have lived side by side, but at times fear and distrust have arisen and religions have fought against each other.

Today, this distrust and violence still exists, but gradually the different religions are trying to work together. On environmental issues, all major faiths now work together to help try to save the planet. On peace, all religions have special programmes on peace education. Where there is fighting, religious leaders now work hard for peace, whereas 50 years ago they would often not even speak to each other.

IS RELIGION DYING OUT?

It was not so long ago that many people thought religion was dying out. Communism had crushed religion in the Soviet Union, and in many parts of the world the old religions seemed to be disappearing. Today, many new religious movements have arisen. Communism has collapsed in many countries, and Christianity and Islam are stronger than before.

At times it can seem as if new religions are appearing every day. Yet most of them have some sort of link to an older religion. For example, in the 19th century, the Mormons, Seventh Day Adventists and Jehovah's Witnesses arose in the USA from Christianity. In Persia, the Baha'i faith came out of Islam. In this century, movements from India and from Hinduism have gone to Europe and America – movements such as Transcendental Meditation, the Hare Krishnas and the Brahma Kumaris. The Unification Church of Korea (the Moonies) has some roots in Christianity, but the Church of Scientology is based on the science fiction of an American writer. All across the world, religions are spinning off new, and at times fascinating, forms.

THE FUTURE OF RELIGION

Religious belief is very strong. It can make a person act kindly or it can lead to acts of great terror. The world's religious leaders are trying to use the power of religion to create peace, justice and respect for our environment.

Each religion is unique, with its own history and beliefs. Each one looks to a different future, but hopefully whatever their viewpoint, they will try to work together on the world problems that face us all.

How many and where?

It is difficult to count the followers of world faiths. The figures given are estimates, and in a few cases even estimates are impossible. The countries listed are those where most followers are found, or where the faith is in a majority.

Buddhism
Probably between 300-400 million, but very difficult to estimate
Asia, especially Myanmar (Burma), Thailand, Cambodia, Laos and Japan

Christianity
Nearly 2 billion
Europe, North and South America, southern Africa and Australasia

Hinduism
Nearly 750 million
India and South Asia

Islam
Over a billion
The Middle East, North and West Africa, South Eastern Europe and South-East Asia

Judaism
12.8 million
North America, Israel and Europe

Sikhism
16 million
Over 80% live in India, mainly in the Punjab in North-West India

Taoism
Numbers impossible to estimate
China and Chinese communities throughout the world

Shinto
Numbers hard to estimate
Only found in Japan

RELIGIOUS FESTIVALS

JANUARY OR FEBRUARY
CHINESE NEW YEAR – *Making sure that the New Year starts with as much good luck as possible. There are many stories about the twelve animal signs.*

FEBRUARY TO APRIL
LENT, GOOD FRIDAY AND EASTER – *Lent lasts for forty days before Easter, and Christians give up something they like during Lent. Good Friday recalls the death of Jesus and Easter his resurrection.*

MARCH *
EID UL ADHA – *The Muslim festival recalling the obedience of Ibrahim and his son Ishmael to the Will of God.*

MARCH AND APRIL
PESAKH (PASSOVER) – *The Jewish celebration of God freeing the Istraelites from slavery in Egypt.*

MARCH AND APRIL
HOLI – *The festival of love and the harvest. It is a light-hearted festival, recalling the amusing tricks that the god Krishna played.*

APRIL 13 (Occasionally April 14)
BAISAKHI – *The Sikh festival that celebrates the founding of the Khalsa. It supports standing up for one's beliefs, and the need to defend the helpless when they are in danger.*

MAY OR JUNE
WESAK – *Buddhists celebrate the three great events in the life of the Buddha: his birth, his enlightenment and his death, which all happened on the same day in different years.*

SEPTEMBER OR OCTOBER
YOM KIPPUR AND ROSH HASHANAH – *Rosh Hashanah is the Jewish New Year. Yom Kippur, nine days later, is a time for remembering the failures and faults of the past year and preparing for a new start.*

OCTOBER OR NOVEMBER
DIVALI – *Celebrates the New Year, and also recalls the story of Rama and Sita from the Ramayana. Oil lamps are lit in the windows of Hindu homes.*

NOVEMBER
Guru Nanak's Birthday – *The births of the founder of Sikhism is celebrated by reading the scripture, the Guru Granth Sahib, by singing the hymns he wrote, and telling stories of him.*

DECEMBER
ADVENT AND CHRISTMAS – *Advent starts four Sundays before Christmas, December 25, which celebrates the birth of Jesus Christ, the Son of God.*

DECEMBER * JANUARY
RAMADAN AND EID UL FITR – *The Muslim period of fasting and subsequent celebration of being a Muslim and living in 'Islam' – submission to Allah.*

* Approximate dates are given, but these do vary as different faiths use different calendars. Muslim dates do not correspond to the solar year at all, but move forward each year. Approximate dates are given at time of publication – these will be about 10 days earlier each year.

GLOSSARY

baptize, baptism The ceremony used when someone becomes a Christian. The new Christian is dipped in water, or water is poured on his head as part of the ritual.

church 1. All Christians 2. A particular group of Christians – either those in one place, or in one denomination, such as the Roman Catholic church or the Anglican church.

crucify A form of execution used in the Roman Empire. The victim was nailed by his hands and feet to a wooden cross and left to die.

disciple Someone who follows a teacher or leader.

enlightened Someone who has 'seen the light', that is, has understood some great truth.

guru The Indian word for a religious teacher. It means 'someone who leads you to the light'.

immortal A person or a god who lives forever.

meditation A way of calming the mind and allowing it to rest on some aspect of belief.

minaret A tall slender tower on an Islamic mosque.

monastery The building where monks or nuns live.

monk A man who gives up marriage and family life to follow his religious faith. Monks are mainly found in the Christian and Buddhist religions.

nun A woman who gives up marriage and family life to follow her religious faith. Nuns are mainly found in Christian and Buddhist religions.

orthodox The word means 'right teaching', but it is particularly used in connection with one branch of Christianity and one tradition of Jewish thought.

pilgrimage A journey for a religious purpose, usually to a special place where some meaningful event took place.

priest Someone who has been specially appointed to perform religious ceremonies.

prophet A person who speaks the word of God, sometimes foretelling the future, sometimes telling people how to live.

sacrifice Giving up something precious. In some regions, birds or animals are killed as an offering to God. This used to be a more common practice than it is now.

sect A small branch of a faith. The word usually refers to a group who hold beliefs that are quite different from most members of that religion.

shrine A small area (a room, or an alcove in a house or small building) set aside to honour one saint or god.

worship A way that is used to honour God. It may be by prayer, singing, or other forms. Worship is a way of showing that God is more important than anything else.

INDEX

Adam and Eve 11,13
Allah 25, 27,46
Americas 14
Amida Buddha 43
Amos 32
apple 11
Asia 14
Asoka, Emperor 6
Australia 3
avatars 19,22

Babylon 33
Baha'i faith 45
Baisakhi 39, 46
bar mitzvah 31 illus
Bethlehem 12
Bhagavad Gita 19, 23
bhakti 23
Bible 11-12, 14-15, 31-32
Brahma 18-19, 22 illus
Brahma Kumaris 45
bread and wine 15

Buddha's footprints, symbol 5-7, 9
Buddhism, Buddhists 3, 4-9, 22 illus, 42-44, 46
Buddhist signposts 8
Burma 6
Byzantium 27

calligraphy 29 illus
Cambodia 6
caste system 21
Chen Buddhism 9, 43
China 6, 9, 14, 27, 42-43
Chinese New Year 42 illus, 46
Christian Aid 44
Christian denominations 17-18
Christianity, Christians 2-3, 10-17, 32, 42, 44-45, 46
Church of Scientology 45
communism 2, 42, 45
Confucianism 42
Covenant 31, 35
creation 11

crescent and star, symbols of Islam 25, 27-29

Dharma 6
disciples 12-13
Divali festival 3, 23 illus, 46
dragon dance 42 illus

Easter 3, 13, 15, 46
Eid ul Adha 46
Eid ul Fitr 46
Europe 45
Exodus 31-32

fish, symbol of Christianity 11-15
Five Ks 41 and illus
Five Pillars of Islam 26
Five Precepts 9
Four Noble Truths 5, 7, 9

Gabriel 11
Gandhi 21

Ganesha 20
Ganges river 21
Garuda bird 19 illus
Genesis 11, 32-33
Golden Temple at Amritsar 41 and illus
Good Friday 13, 46
Gurdwara 41
Guru Amar Das 40
Guru Angad (or Lehna) 38, 40
Guru Arjan 40
Guru Gobind Singh 40
Guru Granth Sahib, Sikh Holy Book 37, 39 and illus, 41, 46
Guru Hargobind 40
Guru Har Krishan 40
Guru Har Raj 40
Guru Nanak 36-38, 40
Guru Ram Das 40
Guru Tegh Bahadur 40

INDEX

hands, Hindu symbol 19-21, 23
Hare Krishnas 45
Hebrew Bible 32
Hijrah 27-28
Hindu holy books 21-22
Hinduism, Hindus 2-3, 18-23, 37, 44-45, 46
Holi festival 20, 46
Holy spirit 14-15
Holy Trinity 14
Hosea 32

imams 2, 29
India 5-6, 14, 19-20, 37
Indus river 19
Ireland 2, 14, 44
Isaiah 12, 32
Islam 24-29, 45, 46
Islamic calendar 27-28
Israel 2, 12, 14, 32-33
Isuzu river 43

Jagannath 20
Japan 6, 9, 42-43, 45
Jehovah's Witnesses 45
Jerusalem 12, 25 illus, 30, 33, 35
Jesus 10-15
Jewish Holy Books 32
Jewish Scriptures on parchment, symbols 31-33, 35
Jews 2, 12-13, 15, 30-35, 45, 46
Jihad 28
Jordan river 32
Joseph 10
Judaism 30-35; see also Jews
Juda Iscariot 13

Ka'ba 26, 28
Kalki 22 illus
karma 7, 20
Kartapur 38
Kaur, Sikh women's surname 41
Khalsa 39, 46
Koran see Qur'an
Krishna 19-20, 22 illus, 23, 46

Kuan Yin, goddess of Mercy 43 illus
K'ung Fu Tzu 42

Lakshmana 23
Lakshmi 19 illus, 20
Lao Tzu 42 illus
Lent 46
Leviticus 32
life after death 11
Luke, Gospel of 12

magi 12
Mahabbharata 23
Makkah (or Mecca) 2, 25-28
Mary, mother of Jesus 10, 11 illus, 13 illus
Matthew, Gospel of 12
Mecca see Makkah
Medina 27, 29
meditation 7
Menorah 30
Messiah 13, 31
Middle Way 5
Mishnah 32 illus
monastery 9, 11 illus
Mool Mantra 37
Moonies see Unification Church of Korea
Mormons 45
Moses 31-32, 35
muezzin 27 illus
Muhammad, Prophet 24-28
Muslims 2, 3, 24-29, 37, 42, 44, 46

Nazareth 12
Nepal 5
New Testament 15
Nile river 32
nirvana 3, 6
Noble Eightfold Path 5, 8, 9
North Africa 14, 27

Old Testament 12, 15, 32
Orthodox Jews 35 illus

Pakistan 19, 37
Paii Canon 6
parables 13
Passover or Pesakh 31, 46
Paul, apostle 14-15
Persia 14, 27, 45
pilgrims at Assissi 44 illus
Pontius Pilate 13
peace 45
prayer mat 25 illus
Protestants 44
Psalms 32
Punjab 37-39
Pure Land Buddhism 43
Puri 20

Qur'an 3, 24, 27-29

Radha 19
Rama 22 illus
Rama and Sita 19, 23, 46
Ramadan 26, 46
Ramayana 19, 23, 46
ram's horn 33
Reform Jews 35 illus
reincarnation 9, 20
religious wars 44
Revelation 15
Rig Veda 19
Roman Catholics 44
Roman Empire, Romans 13-14, 33
Rosh Hashanah 33, 35, 46
Russia 14

Sabbath 2, 13, 30, 33, 34, 35
saint 14
Paint Patrick 14
Sangha 5-6, 9
Sanskrit 21
Saudi Arabia 2, 25
Seventh Day Adventists 45
Shahada 25
Shi'as 28
Shintoism 43, 45

Shinto temple 43 illus
Shiva 20, 22 illus
Siddhartha Gautama 4-6
Sikh gurus 40
Sikhism, Sikhs 36-41, 45, 46
Sinai, Mt 32
Singh, Sikh men's surname 41
South Africa 2, 14
Sri Lanka 6, 23, 44
Sudan 44
Sunnis 28
sword, sikh symbol 37-39, 41
synagogue 33 illus
Syria 14

tallit 35
Talmud 32 illus
Taoism 42-43, 45
Ten Commandments 32, 34
Talwandi 37
Thailand 5 illus, 6-7, 9 illus
Tibet 6
Torah 31 illus, 32 and illus, 33 illus
Transcendental Meditation 45
Tree of the Knowledge of Good and Evil 11

Unification Church of Korea (the Moonies) 45
Upanishads 23

Vedas 23
Vishnu 18-19, 22 illus
Vrindavan 20

Way of the Universe 42
Wesak 46
Western Wall 33, 35 illus, 45 illus

ying and yang, symbols 42-43
yoga 23
Yom Kippur 35, 46
Yugoslavia 2

Zen Buddhism 9, 43

ACKNOWLEDGEMENTS

With thanks to:
Ancient Art & Architecture Collection
Bridgeman Art Library
Circa Photo Library
Colorific!
Douglas Dickens
Eye Ubiquitous
Sonia Halliday Photographs
Hutchison Library
David Midgley
Ann & Bury Peerless
Peter Sanders
Cath Speight
Telegraph Colour Library
World Pictures

Art Direction: *Beverley Speight*
Design: *Nigel Wright*
Editorial Direction: *Liz Dean*
Editor: *Mary Lambert*
Illustration: *Nigel Wright*
Map Illustration: *Ethan Danielson*
Picture Research: *Karen Perryman*
Production: *Graham Saunders*

© 1993 HarperCollins*Publishers* Ltd
First published in 1993. Reprinted 1994, 1996, 1997, 1999

ISBN 000 198359 8

Printed by Printing Express, Hong Kong